FREEDOM OF CHOICE IN HOUSING
Opportunities and Constraints

□□■□□□□■■□□□□□□□□□□□□■□□□■□□□□

ADVISORY COMMITTEE TO THE DEPARTMENT
OF HOUSING AND URBAN DEVELOPMENT

National Academy of Sciences–National Academy of Engineering

Report of the
SOCIAL SCIENCE PANEL

Division of Behavioral Sciences

and the
Recommendations of the
ADVISORY COMMITTEE

NATIONAL ACADEMY OF SCIENCES
NATIONAL ACADEMY OF ENGINEERING
Washington, D.C.   1972

Library of Congress Catalog Card Number 72-75675
ISBN 0-309-02025-5

Available from

Printing and Publishing Office
National Academy of Sciences
2101 Constitution Avenue
Washington, D.C. 20418

Printed in the United States of America

Preface

The Department of Housing and Urban Development, by its legislative mandate, is charged with the attainment of social as well as production objectives in the field of housing. Recognizing the complexity of the task of formulating social policy, it sought to determine the extent of the assured knowledge base from which it might move.

In September 1970, the Department of Housing and Urban Development (HUD) asked the National Academy of Sciences–National Research Council to examine the question of "social mixing" in housing. What knowledge could the behavioral and social sciences bring to bear on the complex problem of social mixing? What has been the experience? Are there feasible programs?

Earlier, in response to a request from the Department, the National Academy of Sciences and the National Academy of Engineering had created an Advisory Committee to HUD. Initially, this Committee was concerned primarily with the technical aspects of Operation Breakthrough, but its area of interest subsequently broadened. In September 1970, at the request of the Department, a Social Science Panel was created and attached to both the Division of Behavioral Sciences of the National Research Council and the Advisory Committee to HUD. The Panel was asked to draw together and assess the behavioral and social science knowledge bearing on the feasibility and desirability of a policy of social mixing, both at the neighborhood level, such as that involved in Operation Breakthrough, and more broadly in metropolitan areas as a whole. Part I is the report of the Social Science Panel.

iii

Utilizing the assessment of the state of the knowledge of the Social Science Panel, the Advisory Committee to HUD, under the chairmanship of George C. McGhee, developed a set of policy and research recommendations, which form Part II of the report.

The Social Science Panel began its deliberations in October 1970. In connection with its assignment, the Panel felt the need for full information regarding HUD's existing policies. At the first meeting of the Panel, it heard from Floyd H. Hyde, Assistant Secretary for Model Cities; Samuel Jackson, Assistant Secretary for Metropolitan Planning and Development; Laurence D. Pearl, Special Assistant to the Assistant Secretary for Equal Opportunity; and Alfred A. Perry, Director of Operation Breakthrough under the Assistant Secretary for Research and Technology. Subsequently, Harold B. Finger, Assistant Secretary for Research and Technology, met with Panel members on a number of occasions. Several other members of the HUD staff, including William Brill, Roland A. Brown, Sandra Sue Brown, Howard Cayton, Robert Colwell, Jean Giuliani, Sybil Phillips, Robert E. Philpott, and Douglas Stenhouse, also made contributions to the Panel's understanding of the Department's operations. The Panel expresses its appreciation for the cooperation of the HUD staff and acknowledges its valuable contribution to the Panel's understanding of the policy context of its work.

The Social Science Panel recognized at the outset of its work the need for a systematic survey of existing knowledge. Housing has not been a major preoccupation of the social sciences; thus the identification and assessment of the relevant knowledge were acknowledged to be difficult and demanding. To accomplish this task, the Panel commissioned five "state of the knowledge" papers, which serve as documentation for the report. Full citations in support of the Panel's findings are to be found in these papers.

The Panel believes that the commissioned papers are a significant contribution in their own right. In the near future they will be published by the National Academy of Sciences under the title *Segregation in Residential Areas.* The papers include "Attitudes on Race and Housing: A Social Psychological View," by Thomas F. Pettigrew, Harvard University; "Institutional and Contextual Factors Affecting the Housing Choices of Minority Residents: The State of Our Knowledge," by Donald L. Foley, University of California at Berkeley; "Social Classes in Cities and Suburbs," by Leo F. Schnore, University of Wisconsin; and "Factors Affecting Racial Mixing in Residential Areas," by James S. Millen, University of North Carolina, prepared under the guidance of the Chairman of the Panel. The fifth paper, "National Housing and Land Use Policy Conflicts: The Social Significance of Operation Breakthrough," by Michael A. Stegman, University of North Carolina, focuses more specifically on the opportunity for social experimentation implicit in programs such as Operation Breakthrough. In addition, the Panel had the benefit of a paper prepared by one of its members, Cora B. Marrett, Western Michigan University, entitled "Social Stratification in Urban Areas."

The Panel is appreciative of the invaluable support for its work provided by the staff of the Division of Behavioral Sciences. Vincent P. Rock served as Executive Secretary for the Panel and assisted in drafting the report. Mrs. Kay C. Harris provided indispensable administrative support. Dr. Henry David, Executive Secretary of the Division, provided valuable suggestions to guide the deliberations of the Panel.

The Panel also acknowledges the significant contribution of the members of the Executive Committee of the Division of Behavioral Sciences: Chairman, James N. Morgan, Institute for Social Research, University of Michigan; Carl A. Auerbach, Law School, University of Minnesota; Alex Inkeles, Graduate School of Education, Stanford University; and Robin M. Williams, Jr., Department of Sociology, Cornell University, who critically reviewed the report and made a number of constructive suggestions.

The term *social mixing* requires clarification. From the perspective of the social sciences, it embraces two different types of questions. On the one hand, there is the question of the degree to which racial and ethnic minorities are interspersed in residential neighborhoods and communities. On the other hand, there is a question of the pattern of stratification of urban areas on the basis of income, occupation, and education. We use the term *racial mixing* in discussing the former question and the term *socioeconomic mixing* in discussing the second.

As the Panel began to examine the research literature, it immediately became clear that research findings are clear and rather conclusive with respect to some aspects of the questions of racial mixing. Along the dimensions of socioeconomic mixing, however, knowledge and information are sparse and far from definitive. The Panel's report reflects its judgment on the reliability of existing knowledge. The primary emphasis is on the forces and experiences in racial integration rather than socioeconomic mixing. The analysis deals mainly with the relationship of blacks and whites. This is a consequence of the sparseness of data on other racial and ethnic groups and of indications from available data that the problem of segregation is more acute among blacks. However, discrimination in housing as based on occupation and economic status has affected members of all non-Caucasian groups living in the United States; blacks, Mexican-Americans, Puerto Ricans, and some ethnic groups of European origin have suffered in the past and often continue to suffer from racial discrimination.

Chapter 1 briefly describes the goals and objectives of H U D and suggests an initial emphasis for a policy of social mixing. Chapter 2 is concerned with existing knowledge of racial mixing at the neighborhood level with special reference to Operation Breakthrough. In Chapter 3, the report moves to the level of the metropolitan housing market and examines what is known about the institutional barriers to open access to housing for all races. In Chapter 4, it turns to an examination of a limited body of research relevant to socioeconomic mixing. Several questions are raised that point to the need for further research to provide a better basis for policy. In Chapter 5, a number of specific suggestions for research are outlined.

AMOS H. HAWLEY
Chapel Hill
January 1972

SOCIAL SCIENCE PANEL OF THE ADVISORY COMMITTEE TO
THE DEPARTMENT OF HOUSING AND URBAN DEVELOPMENT

vii

THE ADVISORY COMMITTEE TO THE DEPARTMENT OF HOUSING AND URBAN DEVELOPMENT

Contents

I REPORT OF THE SOCIAL SCIENCE PANEL

1 Goals and Objectives of the Department of Housing
and Urban Development   3

2 Racial Mixing in Housing at the Neighborhood Level
with Special Reference to Operation Breakthrough   7

Initial Marketing Considerations, 8; "Successful" Interracial
Living, 12; Long-Run Stability, 17

3 The Metropolitan Housing Market: A Web of
Discrimination   20

Private Institutions and the Housing Market, 22: Local
Government and the Housing Supply, 28

4 Socioeconomic Mixing in Metropolitan Areas   32

   Social Stratification in Urban Areas: The Broad Pattern, 33;
   Is Socioeconomic Residential Mixing Desirable?, 35; Is Socioeconomic Residential Mixing Feasible?, 36

5 Urban Development: Research, Evaluation, and
   Experimentation   45

   References   52

II RECOMMENDATIONS OF THE ADVISORY COMMITTEE

   Recommendations of the Advisory Committee to the
   Department of Housing and Urban Development   55

xi

REPORT OF THE
SOCIAL SCIENCE PANEL

1

Goals and Objectives of the Department of Housing and Urban Development

The goals of HUD are set forth in its basic legislation. The 1968 Housing and Urban Development Act and Fair Housing Act

- Reaffirmed the goal of "a decent home and suitable living environment for every American family";
- Directed that "highest priority and emphasis should be given to meeting the housing needs of those families for whom the national goal has not become a reality"; and
- Directed HUD to take "affirmative action" to provide equal opportunity in housing.

At present, there are about 70 million dwelling units in the United States. In 1968, Congress, for the first time, set a target for the following decade of "the construction or rehabilitation of 26 million housing units." In addition, it specified that 6 million of the total should be for "low and moderate income families." Thus, from the standpoint of production, HUD has specific guidelines. Within an overall annual target figure of 2.6 million units, it must aim at the creation of 600,000 for low and moderate income families. Under the Fair Housing Act of 1968, HUD also shares with the Department of Justice responsibility for handling complaints of violations of equal opportunity arising from the 55 million existing housing units covered by that law.

HUD must carry out its responsibilities in an urban environment

3

that is exceedingly complex and subject to rapid change: The nation has continued to become increasingly urbanized—today, two thirds of the population live in the census "urban" places. There has been a steady exodus from the central cities to the metropolitan suburbs, and now more than half of the urban dwellers reside in the suburban rings of metropolitan areas. In the 1960's, in the 200 largest metropolitan areas, the populations of the suburban rings grew five times as fast as those of the central cities. Equally significant, in the same decade, the central cities lost 2.5 million whites and gained 3.0 million blacks. In contrast, the suburbs of the 66 largest metropolitan areas gained 12.5 million whites but only 0.8 million blacks.

Associated with these changes, in many instances, has been a decline in the immediate availability of land suitable for housing in the central cities. Impediments of many kinds exist, including existing buildings, inappropriateness of land plots, the high cost of land assembly, and other market factors. Intergovernmental programs, such as highways and urban renewal, have also tended to reduce land available for housing.

As a general rule, the income of residents of metropolitan areas tends to rise with distance from the center of the principal city in the area. Recently, there have been reported instances of strong resistance by suburbs to low- and moderate-income housing within their boundaries. Many older public housing developments have acquired a negative image as they have filled up with the poorest elements of the minority groups, and this negative image has been used very effectively in resistance to newer forms of publicly assisted housing.

An important consequence of the demographic trends has been to leave the minorities and the poor concentrated in the core areas of central cities. Though they are frequently lumped together, the two groups are very different. Within the minority groups, there is a large and growing middle class still living primarily in the central cities. In absolute terms, the overwhelming number of the poor are white. Nevertheless, the relative incidence of poverty remains much higher among the minority groups.

These facts underline the necessity for the federal government to rationalize housing policy with national urban growth objectives. The legislative mandate to HUD explicitly establishes both production objectives and social objectives. The production targets, especially with respect to low- and moderate-income housing, are higher than in the past. HUD has moved vigorously to achieve these objectives. As it has done so, the necessity to create additional housing outside the central cities, as well as within, has become apparent.

Simultaneously, H U D has sought to carry out the social policy inherent in its mandate. The objectives of its social policy as stated by H U D officials are threefold:

- To increase the housing options of minorities;
- To alter attitudes in directions favorable to desegregation; and
- To improve the general quality of the environment of low and moderate income groups.

The social and production objectives of H U D have led in practice to a commitment to the concept of social mixing in both the suburbs and central cities. Social mixing may mean either racially mixed communities or economically mixed communities or a combination of both. The problems that arise and the attitudes and institutions that must be mobilized to achieve each of these outcomes may be very different. For example, the eradication of racial barriers on the housing market would not necessarily reduce economic stratification. Instead, it could allow middle-class blacks to follow their white counterparts away from the central city. Similarly, an improvement in environmental quality could leave unchanged present socioeconomic patterns since it could involve a mere rebuilding of the neighborhoods where low-income groups presently reside.

In the 1960's the income gap between white and black American families narrowed markedly. Despite the relative improvement in their socioeconomic status, a smaller proportion of minority groups now live in racially mixed neighborhoods than was the case 30 years ago. While racially mixed neighborhoods are numerous and widespread in the United States, available evidence suggests that since 1940 the nation's housing has become more, not less, segregated by race. Segregated housing generally tends to be relatively more costly housing. Thus, to the extent that housing is an important good in itself as well as a factor in the quality of other goods and services, socioeconomic gains are more difficult and more costly for black Americans.

With respect to socioeconomic mixing, it is well known that differences in educational and economic attainment separate people with reference to the opportunities experienced and to future opportunities. The effects are visible in different consumption patterns, avocations, and life styles, in all particulars. There is no reason to assume that the differential influences of socioeconomic levels should operate in one way in a given segment of a population and in another way in the remaining segment of the same population. In fact, there is a very real possibility that blacks and whites of any given socioeconomic level may have more in common than they have with persons of higher or lower levels in their respective color groups.

Moreover, our review of behavioral and social science research supports the view that

- Interracial living is feasible. Evidence to confirm this proposition is both varied and compelling.
- On the other hand, the feasibility of residential mixing of people of different economic levels is uncertain. Our present knowledge in this area is limited.
- Consequently, simultaneous efforts to achieve racial *and* economic mixing may work at cross-purposes.

In light of these considerations, it seems advisable to divide the question of residential mixing and to treat racial and socioeconomic differentials separately. Racial mixing is discussed in Chapters 2 and 3; socioeconomic mixing is examined in Chapter 4.

■□2

Racial Mixing in Housing at the Neighborhood Level with Special Reference to Operation Breakthrough

Operation Breakthrough is a sophisticated effort to advance the systems approach to housing construction and to provide impetus to the acceptance of improved methods of producing and providing housing in the United States. It consists of eight experimental developments in various parts of the country ranging in size from 80 to over 500 units.

Operation Breakthrough, from the viewpoint of social policy, also provides an opportunity to acquire experience relevant to fair housing and equal opportunity policies. Since the nature of Breakthrough's economic structure dictates that housing cost may be fairly uniform around the middle-income range, the questions with which Breakthrough will deal pertain mainly to racial mixing.

Under fair-housing and equal-opportunity laws, Operation Breakthrough will evaluate and oversee the required fair-marketing plans of its developers. HUD officials have made it clear that Breakthrough is committed to the creation of marketing policies that will give equal access to all buyers. At the same time, a major objective is to achieve and maintain a mixed demand so as not to flood the developments with any one racial category of buyer. Overall the aim is a level of buyer satisfaction that will help to validate the marketability of industrialized housing and new residential community land plans.

In seeking to achieve racial mixing in housing, Operation Breakthrough, or, for that matter, the development of any residential neighborhood, must concern itself with three kinds of issues.

7

- What are the marketing considerations in achieving initial interracial mixing?
- What are the requirements for successful interracial living?
- What factors may affect the longer-run stability of interracial residential communities?

The existing research that we have examined throws some light on these questions. On the whole, however, for operational purposes, the research findings are suggestive rather than conclusive. They reinforce our judgment that one of the significant aspects of Operation Break-through ought to be its contribution to knowledge of the require-ments for successful and stable interracial neighborhoods. However, to acquire this vital information, an appropriate research design and necessary support would be required for each project.

INITIAL MARKETING CONSIDERATIONS

In any individual choice of residence, housing quality tends to out-weigh racial prejudice. Studies have shown that positive advantages in a home or neighborhood can offset negative expectations linked to racial mixing. Housing quality and neighborhood quality are per-suasive inducements to the mass of individual customers for housing. Since they apply to members of all racial categories, they can be the basis of common interests where mixed neighborhoods have been established. If mixed housing areas are to generate demand—both white and nonwhite—it is important that they offer better-than-average value for money.

Studies of white buyers of housing in racially mixed areas indi-cate that they are attracted by suitability in location, price, and quality to meet their requirements. Evidence of the importance of general suitability is found in studies of whites who bought in the unpromising situation of older neighborhoods in Philadelphia entered by nonwhites and of white buyers in interracial developments. Some interracial developments have been so "suitable" that white demand has threatened to overbalance nonwhite demand. Home seekers are also concerned with the quality and cost of public services, especially the quality of education and, in some areas, the level of crime.

In addition to any specific set of location and quality factors, the total image conveyed by the individual housing unit and its surround-ing physical and social environment may be significant. The frequent confusion of all forms of government-subsidized housing with the unfavorable image acquired by public housing is a case in point. Housing choice is *par excellence* a decision involving perceptions of status, and one does not accept an inferior situation if there are alternatives. Status considerations help to explain both the importance of quality housing and the resistance to socioeconomic mixing.

In sum, an adequate supply of good-quality housing, which is also a good value for the money, is important in achieving and maintaining racial mixing.

FINDING

> *For both blacks and whites, the quality and convenience of housing and neighborhood services take precedence over racial prejudice in housing decisions.*

*   *   *

The experience of pioneering mixed developments indicates that efforts to appeal to customers with specially favorable attitudes to racial integration, through organizations favoring such policies, are neither successful nor required.

The findings derived from these experiences are reinforced by the shifts in white attitudes over the past generation. Together with a general reduction in antiblack sentiment in numerous realms, trends from 1942 to 1968 show that the attitudes of white Americans toward interracial neighborhoods have become markedly more favorable. Of white respondents to the standard race-and-housing query, the percentage who report that they would not mind black neighbors of the same socioeconomic category more than doubled (from 35 percent to 76 percent). A variety of other survey questions asked at different times by other agencies lead to the same conclusion. The group most responsible for this shift, it should be noted, is composed of post-World War II college-educated whites. In this connection, it is useful to note that the much publicized "white backlash" of the 1960's is not reflected in survey data for the period. While some polarization toward the extremes occurred, the general trend toward pro-desegregation attitudes was maintained. Despite the steady change in attitude, "there remains a significant degree of fear, reluctance, and downright opposition."

It is also useful to take account of the fact that, while the post-World War II college-educated whites have attitudes that are markedly more accepting than other groups, the housing market allows those of higher socioeconomic status to avoid contact with nonwhites more easily than those of lower status. In a study of attitudes in a

racially changing area, high-status whites expressed more favorable
attitudes to nonwhites but were more likely than lower-status whites
to move out of the area. They noted the decline of relative quality
and social standing and had the money to move elsewhere.

Black attitudes tend to support a marketing strategy that provides
equal access to all groups. The overwhelming majority of black Americans assert that they want an opportunity to live in racially mixed
neighborhoods. Survey research contradicts the popular impression
expressed by white Americans that blacks prefer to live in segregated
neighborhoods, and the survey results do not indicate much strength
in the black separatist movement. One important factor in the willingness of blacks to live in mixed neighborhoods is a general commitment to racial harmony. Sizable percentages of blacks report the
belief that a mixed neighborhood provides an opportunity for the
races to learn to get along together. The attitude is reinforced by a
strong desire among blacks to better their housing situations and to
have access to high-quality neighborhood facilities.

However, marketing strategy must take account of the fact that
while most blacks say they want the opportunity to live in a mixed
neighborhood, those who have sought to do so are limited in number. Three main factors seem to account for the present situation:

First, the awareness among blacks of the existing patterns of discrimination is definite and general. The opportunities open to members of different racial categories have been shaped by institutions
responsible for the construction and marketing of most housing. For
example, the choice of locations by developers, generally influenced
by the attitudes of authorities and sources of finance, have favored
segregated housing. They have also reinforced discriminatory marketing practices. In the context of the historical pattern of discrimination, differentiated efforts to attract occupants from different racial
categories will be required. The evidence is that well-conceived approaches can succeed both in the suburbs and in inner-city areas.

A second factor is that, despite the willingness of blacks to live
in mixed neighborhoods, there is skepticism about the net advantage
of mixed residential areas among the young Northerners in the black
community most capable of access to interracial housing. Under the
present circumstances, they are sensitive to incongruities between
the principle and the practice of racial equality. In new developments, a special effort may be warranted to make prospective black
buyers more aware of the existence of policies of nondiscrimination
and of their acceptance by the residents.

In the past, nonwhites of relatively high socioeconomic status have been compelled to accept a dual standard. In search of better housing, they have entered mixed neighborhoods, but these have been mostly in areas whose attraction for higher-status whites was declining. Consequently, these neighborhoods have not been homogeneous in respect to the socioeconomic status of the two racial groups, nonwhites often outranking white residents.

And third, it is important to recognize that there is no widespread desire among black Americans to live in "mostly white areas," to be part of a tiny minority. To the extent that demand exists for interracial living, it is for truly mixed neighborhoods. Moreover, the established trends of nonwhite movement into neighborhoods adjoining those they already occupy will not be altered quickly by a wider range of choice. The consequent changes, even where the quality of property and public services is well maintained and many white residents stay, may continue to be salient enough to discourage white entry.

In sum, even though the black middle class is making significant economic gains, concern about a hostile white reception together with personal and family ties in the black community reinforces black reluctance to move to all-white areas. As a numerical minority, black people (and other minorities) must act from an inferior power position in many situations. Insofar as these are defined on racial lines, they cannot, however, be expected to discard the perceived advantages of communal social and political organizations. In fact, the view that other ethnic groups have been able to exploit communal advantages in the past rests on a very narrow empirical base. Given the adoption of marketing strategies, which evidence a consistent concern for fair housing and equal opportunity, nonwhites are likely to evaluate neighborhoods according to the same criteria as whites and to choose the best housing they can afford. Racial mixing for its own sake is not the chief goal of either group.

FINDING

> *To be successful, a marketing strategy should emphasize the positive racial attitudes that do exist and should take into account the variations in these attitudes. At the same time, the marketing strategy should recognize that there are no clearly identifiable groups holding distinctive racial attitudes with respect to housing.*

"SUCCESSFUL" INTERRACIAL LIVING

Once racial integration is achieved in a project or neighborhood, what are the prospects that it will be successful? Three concepts help to provide the framework for understanding both the possibilities and the requirements for success. They are the following:

- Behavioral change typically precedes rather than follows from attitude change, precisely the opposite process from that frequently assumed to be true.
- Increasing interaction, whether it be of groups or individuals, intensifies and magnifies the processes already under way.
- Positive relationships are encouraged if mutual interests and mutual trust between members of the two groups develop.

Behavior and Attitudes   While behavior and attitudes are in some ways causal in both directions, our view is that, in the area of housing, attitudes are not primarily causal but largely derivative of basic market conditions. This helps to explain the apparent contradiction between rising approval of interracial living by whites and stable black attitudes that favor open housing, on the one hand, and an increased degree of housing segregation, on the other.

Evidence shows that those who have experienced integration previously either as a child or an adult—and particularly as both—are far more likely to move into interracial neighborhoods. White adults who had attended interracial schools as children express more willingness to reside in interracial neighborhoods, as well as other more positive attitudes toward blacks. They were more likely to be living in interracial neighborhoods and to have close black friends than were comparable whites. Likewise, it has been shown that black adults who attended interracial schools as children were more trusting of whites than those who had not had such experience, were more eager for their children to attend desegregated schools, and were more willing to live in interracial neighborhoods even if they would have to "pioneer" to do so. Moreover, the biracially educated blacks were more likely to be living in mostly white neighborhoods, to be sending their children to desegregated schools, and to have close white friends. Thus, interracial experience is a cumulative process for both races, not only within generations but across generations.

Unfortunately, although there are those with previous positive experience with integration, they represent a relatively small proportion of the population. As will be discussed in the following chapter, a web of institutional discrimination has impeded racial mixing in housing. Few households have experience in living in stable interracial neighborhoods. A national study indicated, for example, that only a little over 7 percent of all white urban households were living in neighborhoods that were more than 1 percent black. Even in the North, only about 10 to 15 percent of the whites report a Negro family living in the same block, while in the South the percentage falls to between 3 and 6 percent.

In the absence of experience with stable interracial living, attitudes may impede the initial phases of integration and in one important respect: Many white Americans confuse socioeconomic class differences with race. Consequently, class characteristics are often attributed to race. To illustrate, when a new white neighbor moves into a white block, he may typically be assumed to be similar in outlook and status until he proves otherwise. But when a new black moves into a previously white block, he may typically be assumed to be different in outlook and status until he proves otherwise. In other words, whites commonly perceive blacks as holding contrasting beliefs. It is this racist perception and not race *per se* that leads to resistance.

Interaction—Positive or Negative   Interaction between two groups may provide an increased basis for trust or may escalate distrust. In either case, an increase in interaction, whether it be of groups or individuals, magnifies the ongoing processes. The common view that more contact among blacks and whites will solve the nation's racial difficulties is a gross oversimplification. It is no more true than the assertion that contact invariably increases intergroup hostility. Interracial contact can lead either to greater prejudice and rejection or to greater respect and acceptance, depending on the situation in which it occurs. Residential neighborhoods may not only involve relatively intense interactions but are perceived as having aspects of intimacy that present particularly sensitive contact situations.

Some of the earliest and most systematic studies of reactions to racial mixing were made in public housing projects. One major study by Deutsch and Collins took advantage of a made-to-order social experiment in the late 1940's. In accordance with state law, two public housing projects in New York City were desegregated; in all cases, apartment assignments were made irrespective of race or personal preference. In two other comparable projects in Newark, New Jersey, the two races were assigned to separate buildings. Striking differences were noted between the attitudes toward blacks of white housewives in the desegregated and the segregated developments. The desegregated women held their black neighbors in higher esteem and were considerably more in favor of interracial housing (75 percent to 25 percent). They had more direct contact with blacks in optimum situations—as neighbors in the same building, outside in common open spaces, and at laundry and grocery facilities. When asked to name the chief fault of blacks, they mentioned such personal problems as feelings of inferiority and oversensitivity; by contrast, the segregated women listed such qualities as trouble-making, rowdy, and dangerous. These differences in attitude stem from the fact that the desegregated housewives more often viewed blacks as individuals and as people like themselves.

In the intervening decades, nonwhite demand for low-cost housing, especially in the larger cities, has been greater than that of whites. Fears of declining amenities, of crime, and of racial conflict have become more marked. At the same time, studies of private interracial housing at a variety of price levels, including partially subsidized moderate-income housing, tend to confirm the positive possibilities of residential racial mixing in reducing prejudice. In sum, we concur with Pettigrew's conclusion that "an effective way to alter opposition, white and black, to interracial housing is to have them live successfully in such housing."

Constructive Contact   If interaction may intensify either trust or mistrust, what are the essential requirements for constructive contact? Nearly two decades ago, G. W. Allport identified four characteristics of contact situations that are of utmost importance if prejudice is to be lessened when members of two groups interact. They are, in our view, directly relevant to the problems of racial mixing at the housing-project or neighborhood level. Based on his review of the relevant literature, Allport concluded that for constructive contact to occur two groups must share four attributes:

- Equal status,
- Common goals,
- Interdependence, and
- The support of authority.

While the major operational implications of the attributes of a constructive contact situation are reasonably well understood, their application in a particular project or neighborhood remains more art than science.

What does it mean to possess equal status? Clearly in the past there was considerable interracial contact. However, most blacks encountered by whites were servants, field hands, and low-status service workers. Such black professionals as existed remained within the black community where whites rarely met them. There was only very limited equal-status contact and very little change in the degree of interracial understanding. In contrast, the recent increase in college-educated blacks who have moved into positions of responsibility in many occupations is producing a significant increase in equal-status contact in the employment situation. And in a wider sense, as the average black income more nearly approaches that of whites, an even broader range of equal-status contact becomes possible, since income is a most powerful surrogate for the more intangible aspects of status.

In an objective sense, equal status refers to individuals or groups with similar incomes, education, and occupation. In a more subjective sense, it connotes the ability of people to interact as equals in a situation. People of equal status in the objective sense are more likely than others to possess congruent outlooks and beliefs. And as they come in contact, congruence is more likely to be mutually perceived. To the degree that negative feeling about the effect of racial mixing on the quality and status of a neighborhood remains, it can be reduced by similarity in other social characteristics. A number of studies of the reactions of white residents to nonwhite entrants in a neighborhood record the effect of perceived similarity of status and life style in overcoming initial reserve. Subjectively, of course, equal status in a situation structured in one way may not hold to the same degree for a situation structured in another way. The point here is that, having attracted whites and nonwhites with common positions in society, the design and management of housing development should, as far as is feasible, seek to reinforce the initial sense of equal status. Direct observation of the status characteristics of other entrants of a different race is less easy for prospective customers evaluating a new development. Uniformity in the cost of housing units can help allay anxiety about association with low-status neighbors.

Another way in which a sense of equal status may be reinforced is by continuing emphasis on the common goals sought by both groups. The most obvious of these has been mentioned previously: good quality housing in an attractive neighborhood. But there may be others of importance—safety and control of crime, for example.

Surveys show that blacks are even more concerned about crime than are whites. Security at home and on the streets is a common goal of the vast majority of both groups.

Good-quality schools and efficient public services of various kinds are not only shared goals, but they also tend to require cooperative interdependent action for their attainment. Contact arising naturally from the pursuit of common interests is perhaps the most powerful solvent of prejudice. There is a sense in which a neighborhood needs problems amenable to effective mutual action if the dynamic process of integration is to work. However, housing management should avoid situations in which competition takes place along strictly racial lines.

Finally, a neighborhood needs the sense that interracial contact has the explicit support of custom, law, or authority. The vital role played in race relations by the social climate is difficult to over-emphasize. Support may derive from many different sources. For example, it may be provided by the actions of the developer, by local citizens' groups, by the government, or by all three. Congress, in the Fair Housing Act of 1968, of course, provided explicit sanction and gave HUD responsibility for exerting leadership.

In the case of Operation Breakthrough, the developer is expected to market and monitor the project in a manner that provides visible sanction for interracial living. In addition, he may be well advised to facilitate the creation of neighborhood organizations whose norms also sanction interracial contact. Lack of such organizations in established neighborhoods has slowed the progress of integration in housing. A small number of residents who are particularly hostile or sympathetic to the minority group can guide the reaction of the hesitant majority and so impede or facilitate racial mixing.

Positive racial relations in one area of life are not always transferable to tolerant behavior in new situations. For example, good working relations are not directly transferable to easy acceptance of integrated residential living. There may be intervening variables. Consider the apparent inconsistencies of a neighborhood group of white steel workers in the Chicago area. These men were all members of the same thoroughly desegregated union and all worked in desegregated plants. In fact, elected positions such as shop steward, executive board member, and vice-president of the union were held by blacks, who shared with whites the same locker rooms, lunch rooms, showers, and toilets in both the union hall and the plants. Only 12 percent of the whites studied evidenced a "low acceptance" of blacks in the work situation, and the deeper their involvement in union activities, the greater their acceptance of blacks as co-workers. Neighborhood acceptance, on the other hand, was a vastly different matter. Bolstered by a neighborhood organization that opposed desegregation, 86 percent of the white workers rejected the idea of allowing blacks to live near them. It was further noted that those men most involved in the collective existence of the neighborhood rejected the idea most adamantly. The effects of interracial contact at work did not extend to housing.

One key to understanding this process is the operation of the institutions in each of these situations. Most of the steel workers, like members of society in general, tend to act in ways that are expected of them, even when these expectations counter one another. Thus, the inconsistency is more apparent than real. It appears conflicting to the observer, but to the person involved his behavior is perfectly reasonable. In both situations, he is living by the norms of the groups to which he refers his behavior—his reference groups.

Finally, of course, government provides the ultimate source of authoritative support for a policy of racial mixing. Here the proposition stressed at the beginning of this section—that behavioral change typically precedes rather than follows attitude change—provides a key to the proper policy posture. The goal ought to be to achieve increased opportunity for racial mixing without placing undue emphasis on hostile white attitudes. This would, of course, imply reliable and effective enforcement procedures. In sum, the effective way to alter opposition, white and minority, to interracial housing is to provide the opportunity for both groups to gain experience in successful racially mixed residential areas. Carefully evaluated experiments are needed to provide practical knowledge of how to achieve this objective.

FINDING

> *Attitude changes are effected where the physical and social conditions encourage and support behavioral changes.*

*   *   *

LONG-RUN STABILITY

Even when "successful" residential mixing at the neighborhood level is achieved, the probability of longer-run stability is frequently uncertain. The stability of mixed neighborhoods depends on a continuing balance in the racial proportions between the initial residents and the new entrants. In a highly mobile population, small differences in residential preference may be reflected in slightly different rates of movement into and out of a particular neighborhood by white and non-white populations. If a higher percentage of new entrants than of residents are of one racial category, the neighborhood is, in a crucial sense, unstable.

Racial transition is not inevitable, however, even when the new entrants are for a time predominantly from one group. Stability may ultimately be achieved at a new level of racial mix as the ratios of new entrants to existing residents become similar.

Complete racial transition occurs if the demand for homes by a previous minority in the area is large enough to absorb all the properties that become available in the neighborhood. Substantial transitions have taken place in the past, especially in inner-city neighborhoods. Such transitions may gradually become less frequent as nonwhite demand is dispersed over more areas and over wider price ranges. However, for the medium term at least, most residential change is likely to result from the "filtering down" process by which homes and neighborhoods successively meet the needs of less affluent occupants as those with the means to do so move on to new property. The process may be expected to result in a changing racial mixture in many neighborhoods and complete transition in some.

In some circumstances, practically no level of minority-group occupancy may be low enough to ensure the stability of a mixed neighborhood. In other cases, neighborhoods may be stable even though the ratio of nonwhites to whites is very high.

In the view of many proponents of integrated housing, the neighborhood with 10 to 30 percent nonwhites deserves particular attention. In the short run, however, neighborhoods with less than 2 percent nonwhites, now relatively widespread, may be a necessary step in the enlargement of minority-group opportunities. Obviously, the latter level of racial mixing cannot provide equal access, nor does it ensure a swift and smooth advance to more substantial integration.

For the medium-term future, the continued growth in the non-white population, improvements in the provision of equal access to housing, and the relative rise in the economic status of nonwhites are all likely to contribute to a changing composition in many neighborhoods. Instability will, of course, occur when minority demand is concentrated in particular neighborhoods. Also important in the pattern and rate of change is the reaction of existing residents and, even more, that of the prospective entrants belonging to the racial category that formerly provided the most entrants. If white demand is reduced significantly, for example, then even a moderate level of nonwhite demand may absorb all the housing units coming on the market in a particular neighborhood. This phenomenon can occur at very low levels of nonwhite occupancy. As it does, expectations among whites may become less favorable and a transition process may be accelerated. Alternatively, if demand from the nonwhites falls off, is diverted elsewhere, or is controlled, stability at a new level may be achieved and the transition postponed. Demand from whites may drop as the proportion of nonwhites rises, but no proportion of nonwhites is so large as to make stability within a development impossible. There is no consistent evidence to identify a particular "scare point" at which whites will flee or refuse to enter; too much depends on local circumstances.

Since the process of residential choice is dynamic and complex, the opportunities for effective managerial intervention to maintain stable racially mixed neighborhoods are numerous. However, effective intervention depends on a realistic assessment of the supply and demand factors in the situation as well as an awareness of the role of prejudice in shaping the market. In fact, there is considerable evidence that the management policies of those who rent or sell housing do influence stability and racial proportions in various areas. For example, control of racial proportions appears to be commonplace in mixed rental developments. Control can be maintained without the use of formal quotas by the screening of applicants, or more acceptably, by varying the level of promotion to different racial groups. When a policy of this kind merely involves the reversal of the more usual practice of marketing to only one racial category, objections are likely to be minimal. Deliberate manipulation of demand in particular developments is also accepted by members of all racial categories, if they are anxious to maintain racial mixing. In one view, intervention to maintain stable racially mixed neighborhoods is an essential counterweight to the present prevalent pattern of institutional discrimination, which is discussed in the next chapter. Open access in a free market is the ultimate objective. Meanwhile, progress toward equal opportunity may require countervailing intervention to offset the effects of discrimination. In this respect, it should be noted that the constitutionality of "benign quotas" has not yet been settled by the Supreme Court.

FINDING

> *There is no ratio of blacks to whites that is known to ensure success in racial mixing. The ratios or proportions must be adapted to the particular populations involved.*

□□■3

The Metropolitan
Housing Market:
A Web of Discrimination

Today, in many metropolitan areas there are in fact two housing markets, not one. A web of institutional discrimination exists that reduces the "effective" supply, especially for nonwhite minorities. The institutional web, comprised of many interrelated components, ranges from the services of realtors, mortgage lenders, appraisers, and developers; to the laws, government regulations, and administrative and political behavior of government officials; to patterns and practices related to employment, schools, transportation, and community services.

The objective of housing policy over the long run ought to be a single housing market in each metropolitan area with equal access for all races. This objective, because of the dynamic nature of the housing market, does not imply less diversity among neighborhoods. If anything, the diversity may increase. Moreover, it suggests that limits on the stability of mixed neighborhoods will persist.

At the same time, it is essential to accept the fact that stable, racially mixed neighborhoods must become much more common if equal opportunity in housing is to become a reality. To this end, efforts to revitalize the inner city still deserve careful attention. Neighborhoods with special social or economic attractions inhabited by a nonwhite majority but having a stable white minority are achievable. Such neighborhoods could help preserve the institutions and political strength of black people, while reducing their isolation. In our con-

20

sidered view, however, there must also be increased opportunity for minority movement to suburban areas of varying price levels and social character, where the largest proportion of white America now lives. Such areas have attracted white people for positive reasons— better housing, more space, new communal facilities, access to employment—not predominantly as a refuge from black invasion of the cities. It must be expected that suburban areas will appeal to an increasing number of black people for the same reasons.

A strategy that takes account of the dynamic character of the housing market and facilitates the desired changes is necessary. The pattern of residential distribution is affected by the interplay of many different market factors. The relative strength and concentration of demand among different income groups and among the white majority and the minorities are of key importance. Changes in income distribution and housing preferences play a role. The desire to maintain racial or ethnic cohesion is a factor. And influencing every aspect of the market process is the level of tolerance or of prejudice within the metropolitan area as a whole, as well as in individual communities. Two additional sets of factors deserve special attention both because of their intrinsic importance and because they are amenable to modification in the medium term. These are

- The supply of housing, that is, the actual physical supply, but especially the "effective" supply that is presently constrained by an array of institutional barriers to equal access; and
- The policies of governments—local, state, and federal—that impede or facilitate the creation of an adequate supply of housing and equal access to it.

Improvement in the performance of metropolitan housing markets to provide equal access to an adequate supply of housing is a complex and continuing process. There are, in our view, three essential requirements. First, the federal government must perfect a coherent strategy that takes account of the interplay of the multiple factors at work. Second, authoritative sanction for equal access must be provided by enforcement of the law to a single standard. Third, measures must be devised to reduce specific private and public barriers to equal access to an adequate supply of housing. The specific barriers are considered in the subsequent sections. Here, we emphasize the importance of the following general finding with respect to the performance of metropolitan housing markets.

Any fragmentation of the housing market constitutes a basis for segregation. Multiple autonomous governments and private institutional barriers contribute to fragmentation.

*   *   *

PRIVATE INSTITUTIONS AND THE HOUSING MARKET

Housing is produced and marketed primarily by the private sector. Institutional factors differ depending on whether the housing units are part of the existing stock or the result of new developments and on whether the property is offered for sale or rent. In the following sections, the role of real estate brokers and boards, the management of rental properties, the developers of new property, and mortgage-lending agencies are considered in turn. Last, there is a brief discussion of the present status of the restrictive covenant.

Real Estate Brokers and Real Estate Boards   The National Association of Real Estate Boards (NAREB) has publicly stated that all realtors are expected to conform to the fair housing laws. However, there is some evidence that the brokers have been learning how to continue their screening activities, but with greater care so that they are not caught openly in violation of the new legislation.

Most of the sales of older houses are handled through real estate brokers. The broker paired with an owner may provide a formidable gatekeeping arrangement. The seller may feel a sense of responsibility on behalf of his majority-white neighbors and may determine almost as a matter of course to instruct the realtor not to consider "undesirable" prospects. The real estate broker, in addition to a loyalty to the seller, may have an eye to future business and may interpret his "professional" responsibility as maintenance of the neighborhood *status quo.*

Every routine act, every bit of ritual in the sale or rental of a dwelling unit can be performed in a way calculated to make it either difficult or impossible to consummate a deal.[1]

Majority white persons are able to spend a long period searching for housing and can expect the cooperation of a real estate broker; they are not screened until financial negotiations begin. But minority prospects may be screened at the very start before a broker even expresses willingness to be of direct assistance. Various delaying tactics may be employed by the broker. For example, the broker may delay the submission of the client's order or find technical difficulties. The difficulties are reflected in the fact that two thirds of the black adult population say they expect difficulties to be created by some white person when looking for a house. Twice as many blacks believe real estate companies are harmful to their rights as find them helpful.

The expectation that property values will decline steeply as a consequence of nonwhite entry in a neighborhood was long common among home owners and some professionally engaged in the housing market. In some instances, sharp fluctuations in house prices have occurred immediately following nonwhite entry. However, the weight of the evidence is that, in comparison with all-white neighborhoods of otherwise similar character (age, location, housing quality, etc.), property values in neighborhoods entered by nonwhites do not generally fall and have sometimes risen because of the concentration of nonwhite demand.

When it becomes apparent that a particular neighborhood is undergoing change, [real estate agents] are in a position to either speed up or slow down the process. It has been the pattern throughout the country for real estate interests to play an extremely destructive role in relation to interracial communities. They spread misinformation about declining values in changing neighborhoods, using it to manipulate desegregation and "resegregation" by causing a rapid turnover once Negro families have started to move in. In some cases, they simply do not show houses in one section to prosective Negro buyers, nor houses in another section to whites; at times they use genuine scare tactics to speed up turnover to their own advantage.[2]

Panic selling, it must be noted, however, has not been general even in those areas in which racial transition has been progressing.

Real estate brokers in a given community are normally members of a real estate board. Real estate boards and the housing information systems they operate could play an important role in achieving and maintaining a single integrated housing market throughout a metropolitan area. However, at present these institutions frequently work at odds with this goal. Sale of housing to minorities is affected by the multiple-listing practices of real estate boards. A broker is normally on the distribution list for listings produced by his own real estate board. But he only has access to the listings produced by other boards if he can establish reciprocity with brokers on them or if he can take out a nonresident membership. Real estate boards have typically resisted taking in minority persons as brokers. Memberships have not been available to nonresident minority brokers in all-white surburban real estate boards. A minority broker therefore has great difficulty in providing the full range of listings available in suburban areas to a minority client, and the client is at the mercy of majority-white brokers in these suburbs. Thus, listing practices may "effectively bar minority people looking for housing from having access to indispensable information about what is offered."

FINDING

> *Even in the absence of multiple autonomous governments, the lack of adequate mechanisms for the distribution of housing information among realtors and home seekers tends to fragment a housing market.*

*   *   *

Role of Management in Rental Housing   Rental housing, no matter how desirable and advantageous home ownership may be, remains the immediate prospect for most minority families. Rental housing has provided a way for many nonwhites to obtain newer homes in mixed neighborhoods. This view gains support from the findings of Sudman *et al.* that integrated neighborhoods have a higher proportion of renters than segregated ones and that nonwhites are more likely than whites to be renters in these neighborhoods. The sense of uncertainty that both whites and nonwhites may feel in entering a mixed neighborhood may be less pronounced in the case of rental housing since no large investment is involved.

Managers of rental property are more open to pressure and persuasion than are a multitude of individual home owners and, once racial mixing is accepted, they can do much to ensure its stability. On the one hand, the influence of central management of a group of rental properties can be used to facilitate entry by members of different racial groups, can help create an atmosphere in which racial mixing is regarded as normal and initial frictions are overcome, and can maintain a housing environment that will attract different races on grounds of quality or value for money. On the other hand, since the turnover in rental property is usually greater than in owner-occupied housing, where management is ineffective or decides to promote a transition from white to nonwhite occupancy, extreme instability is more likely than in an owner-occupied area. Of course, in some instances turnover can also be used to restore racial balance as was demonstrated by the new management of a California development in which the racial composition was changed from 100 percent black to approximately 60 percent white and 40 percent black.

A considerable volume of good-quality rental housing convenient to new employment opportunities has been built in the last decade. For example, a great increase in the construction of new apartments has taken place in the suburbs since 1950. Better housing and more services for the rental dollar are offered in the suburbs than are available in the central city. Unfortunately, of course, informal discrimination is still widely prevalent in the letting of rental properties.

Landlords, whether apartment owners or managers, act as gatekeepers to their apartment buildings and immediate neighborhoods for various reasons: They may live there themselves and wish to screen their own prospective neighbors; they may seek to protect what they take to be the interests of present or prospective majority-white tenants; they may be unfavorably influenced by stereotypes about housing maintenance by minority tenants; and they may believe that minority households, once admitted, will stimulate pressures for further minority tenancy. As a result of such discrimination and of housing shortages in areas adjacent to the inner city, minority households are victims of an unusually tight market—actually, a submarket. And, of course, the newer apartments are generally located in predominantly white or all-white residential areas and are even more likely to discriminate against prospective minority tenants than older apartment buildings in or closer to the inner city.

FINDING

> *Experience demonstrates that success in racial mixing in rental properties is influenced in considerable degree by the attitudes, the skill, and the wisdom of property managers.*

*   *   *

Role of Developers in the Sale of New Housing   In earlier periods, the sale of new housing, particularly tract housing built by large developers, was subject to prevalent discriminatory practices. Cases of exclusion of minorities from large suburban developments are known; once forced, some of these have been smoothly integrated. Large firms of home builders, in particular, have been changing their practices. In some areas

... minority prospects appear to get much better treatment from tract builders with their own sales forces than from realtors. To some extent this is due to the differences in marketing factors, i.e.:

(1) The prospective transports himself to the site and needs very little service from the sales agent on the premises.

(2) The price and terms are usually fixed and widely advertised, so that there is very little room for bargaining.

In addition, there seems to be no organized resistance from the home building industry, as there obviously is within the fields dominated by NAREB (National Association of Real Estate Boards). In our judgment, the different attitudes of white realtors and white home builders is at least partially a reflection of the fact that the National Association of Home Builders has a more favorable attitude toward residential integration than does NAREB.[3]

In new developments, a pattern of total minority exclusion, once established, is extremely difficult to change. Alternatively, a pattern of racial mixture, once established, may enhance the probability that integration within a development will continue. In this context, changes in the policies of large developers can be of great significance. If the developer decides to pursue a positive policy of marketing open occupancy, large sources of new buildings are opened to minority group members who can afford to buy. This is now happening in many areas, and the volume of housing thus made available for mixed occupancy helps to overcome the problem of concentrated demand from middle-income nonwhites, which, in some instances, faced pioneer developers of private mixed neighborhoods. However, progress in other sectors of the market is also essential to open up opportunities for minority families along the chain of moves resulting from the occupancy of new housing.

FINDING

> *New, large-scale developments of residential properties for sale have been more amenable to racial mixing than have been older housing units widely scattered in established neighborhoods. Factors of importance in this respect appear to be (1) the central control of sales policy, (2) the strong market orientation of the home building industry, and (3) the absence of precedent in the newly created developments.*

*   *   *

Mortgage Financing The unwillingness of many financial institutions to advance money to nonwhites for the purchase of homes in mainly white areas continues to constitute a barrier to blacks otherwise able to compete with whites for financing. The situation has been described in the following terms:

Mortgage and credit is the key to acquisition of good housing via home owner-ship. . . . Whites and non-whites of comparable economic status and owning simi-lar properties seem to receive, on the whole, similar treatment from most lending agencies, with the crucial exception: institutional lenders traditionally have re-quired properties for non-white occupancy to be located in recognized minority residence areas, and many lenders continue to enforce this special requirement. By making mortgage credit available to minorities in certain areas and withhold-ing it in others, lending agencies help to maintain segregation.[4]

Based on our discussions with black brokers and fair housing brokers we believe it is fair to say that minority people trying to move out of the ghetto have *even* more trouble than formerly in obtaining mortgage loans. Earmarking "minority mortgage money" for loans on so-called ghetto property means that minority applicants are more likely than ever to find it hard to get loans for purchase in suburban areas.[5]

Achievement of a significant increase in racially mixed neighbor-hoods requires no less than a complete reversal in past mortgage-financing practices, which have required properties for nonwhite occupancy to be located in recognized minority residence areas.

FINDING

> *Mortgage financing institutions have had separate lending policies for blacks and for whites. They have been timid in developing policies for realizing mixed residential areas.*

*   *   *

Restrictive Covenant or Deed Restriction   Probably no institutional device has been more deeply woven into the practices bearing on the rental and sale of real estate than the restrictive covenant or deed re-striction. Even though the courts no longer enforce them, full up-to-date evidence is lacking about how these covenants are interpreted by prospective sellers, buyers, and others involved in the complex pro-cess of transferring property. It is quite possible that a large number of persons use the covenants to maintain discrimination. We share the view of one observer who said: "Most commentators today are of the opinion that such a covenant is illegal and should be regarded so, rather than accepting the incongruous fiction that it is legal but un-enforceable." Although many state laws outlaw the making of restric-tive covenants, the effects of the persisting ambiguity in other states

with respect to restrictive covenants runs counter to the objective of
racial mixing and should be eliminated.

FINDING

> *Despite the Supreme Court decision regarding the nonen-
> forceability of restrictive covenants, there is reason to believe
> that such covenants continue to have some effect in prevent-
> ing the development of interracial neighborhoods.*

*   *   *

LOCAL GOVERNMENT AND THE HOUSING SUPPLY

The supply of housing is influenced by the actions, both positive and
negative, of local governments. Land-use planning, zoning, and other
measures in effect shape the pattern and character of housing development and utilization in a metropolitan area. Scarcity of suitable
land for housing in the central city may compel movement outward
or upward. Suburbs, in an effort to maintain their present status, may
seek to restrict the creation of moderate and low-cost housing. Costs
of rehabilitation and maintenance to comply with local standards may
lead to abandonment of properties. And, in the entire process of
change, lack of power at the metropolitan level, when coupled with
many parochial autonomous units, may aggravate the fragmentation
of the housing market—one set for whites and one set for minorities—
with a limited number of areas in transition and an even smaller number that are racially mixed and stable. In this outcome, a lack of
coherence and equity in the distribution of the public costs and
benefits of metropolitan living play an important role.

Control of Land Use   Historically, control over land use has been
delegated by the states to local units of government. As the growing
urban population spread out beyond the central cities, creating metropolitan areas, control over land use became an even more critical
and strategic function. In most parts of the country and in most
metropolitan areas, the exercise of land-use controls has continued
to be divided among scores, sometimes hundreds, of local units of
government.

As urbanization increased, land suitable for housing in the central
cities tended to become scarce. Increasingly, housing construction
has taken place outside in the suburban rings. Local governments
have commonly used a number of their delegated powers over land

use and construction to resist initiatives they viewed as leading to "social mixing," whether racial or economic. Ironically, civic reforms have frequently been converted into mechanisms for preserving the *status quo*. This has been particularly true of zoning and also, to a degree, of urban planning.

Land-Use Plans   The land-use plan of a municipality, a county or a metropolitan-level government or quasi government identifies certain community or regional goals and presents a map-like diagram of the arrangement of future land uses that will foster or incorporate these goals. Most local governments with populations exceeding 5,000 now have planning boards and land-use plans. Until recently, these plans have focused almost completely on physical objectives. Social and political presumptions and goals have not been openly stated or related to physical plans.

Most land-use plans take a conserving or preserving approach. They may concentrate on the major goal of "orderly development" and such further subgoals as the control of residential densities, the preservation of open space, and the deliberate containment of commercial and industrial land uses. The plans have rarely sought to deal directly with housing requirements. They tend to reflect (1) community sentiment and leaders' commitment to prevent the influx of minority households or, perhaps more commonly, to discourage the influx of low- and even moderate-income households; (2) the structure of local government in which a housing authority and a renewal agency may be operating relatively independently from the planning department; and (3) a tendency of land-use plans to be more concerned with the elimination of blight than with the positive provision of housing for families not well served by the existing housing market.

Zoning   Zoning is unquestionably at the very center of the process of land-use control. It is thus at the center of major value conflicts, for, as some gain what they seek, others lose. Zoning has been so completely incorporated into the local political process and has become so well understood by the citizenry (at least with respect to its broad possibilities) that it is probably the major mode of land-use regulation relied on by politicians and residents. More communities have zoning ordinances than have planning boards and a considerably larger number have zoning ordinances than have land-use plans.

Zoning purports to control the character of physical development and to ensure orderly development on behalf of the community as a whole. Thus, it regulates type of land use, lot size, setback, parking requirements, etc. Indirectly it controls density of development and thus assists in ensuring that services can be properly related, that traffic can be accommodated, and that timing of development can be effectively controlled. By its very nature, zoning is exclusionary. Most studies rank zoning as a very significant device for exclusion.

The nature of zoning is such that it is difficult to disentangle its control over physical development and land use *per se,* its influence over the economic status of prospective residents, and its use to discriminate against specific ethnic or racial groups. Babcock concludes his long treatment of zoning with the judgment: ". . . social influences, far more than economic considerations, motivate the public decision makers in zoning matters."

Subdivision Regulation   Another important type of land-use control used by local governments is subdivision regulation. The planning commission must approve the proposed design of a subdivision; thus, it can exercise control over the process by which land is converted into building sites. Over 80 percent of the communities having zoning also have subdivision regulations.

> . . . the plat approval agency may through a process of negotiation persuade a developer to include detailed regulations governing the siting of structures, landscaping, architectural design, and so forth, tailored to the particular needs of his subdivision, which it could not easily require in its general [public] regulations.[6]

Local governments have commonly used a number of their delegated powers over land use and construction to resist initiatives that they view as leading to social mixing, whether racial or economic. These include

• Land-use plans that have tended to focus on "physical development" and have rarely sought to deal directly with housing requirements;
• Zoning in which social influences, more than economic considerations, motivate public decision makers; and
• Subdivision regulation that controls the process by which land is converted to building sites.

Traditionally, the right of local communities to determine their own land use has been accepted. However, it is virtually impossible for individual local communities to deal effectively with social problems that are metropolitan in scope, such as housing discrimination against minorities or an inadequate supply of low- and medium-cost housing. As these problems have become acute, local control of land use has come under review. The Housing and Urban Development Act of 1968, for example, required all local communities to identify and to take into account the housing needs of both the region and the local communities, with a subgoal of encouraging each community to do its share in providing housing for disadvantaged households. In 1970, the President's Task Force on Urban Renewal suggested "that federal aids of all sorts be withdrawn from communities unless they undertake a program to expand the supply of low- and moderate-cost housing within their boundaries." There have also been proposals for the fiscal assistance, review of development and zoning policies, and increased incentives for participation in remedial programs.

In our view, a new balance needs to be struck between local rights and metropolitan needs in the housing field. This will require that ultimate responsibility for the supply of housing be located at the metropolitan level. At the same time, the exercise of authority at that level ought to reflect a creative search for solutions that satisfy the need for housing without abrogating the right of local choice. The operational objective is a new context within which local decisions are made.

FINDING

> *It is unlikely that a policy of racial mixing can be consistently applied in metropolitan areas in which there are two or more autonomous governments. For any one locality to act in the total social interest is for it to put itself in a position to be beggared by others who do not accept similar responsibility voluntarily.*

□■□■4

Socioeconomic Mixing
in Metropolitan Areas

In the first half of the nineteenth century, spatial separation of residences along socioeconomic class lines was not common in American
cities. In the second half of the century, land-use differentiation in-
tensified, but the large immigrant populations were fairly evenly
distributed among native-born urban populations, except as the new-
comers were concentrated among the lower socioeconomic strata.
The small black populations of the northern cities, however, were
much more confined residentially than the foreign-born elements.

In the twentieth century, American cities have been characterized
by residential stratification along socioeconomic class lines. From
time to time the separation of socioeconomic groups in society as
a whole, and in the cities in particular, has been challenged and im-
pugned. To avoid confusion, it is useful to differentiate issues of class
from those of race. Recently, for example, discussions of the "urban
crisis" and the relationship of cities and suburbs have tended to confuse issues of color and class that are essentially separable.

Undoubtedly, socioeconomic and racial movements in the population do at times converge. During and after the two world wars, large
numbers of migrants to the central cities were not only poor but
black. Nevertheless, for an understanding of social stratification in
urban areas—ranking groups on the basis, generally, of income, education, and occupation—it is necessary to differentiate between race
and class, and sometimes even between different parts of the country.

In their study of Negroes, the Taeubers found, in 207 cities studied,

32

three fifths or more of the Negro residents would have to be relocated to achieve an unsegregated distribution. However, they concluded that

...the net effect of economic factors in explaining (racial) residential segregation is slight. . . . Clearly, residential segregation is a more tenacious social problem than economic discrimination. Improving the economic status of Negroes is unlikely by itself to alter prevailing patterns of racial residential segregation.[7]

Moreover, it follows that, without measures to reduce racial discrimination, housing assistance for low-income families could tend to increase segregation. One effect of housing subsidies may be to increase the mobility of lower-income white families and enable them to emulate the segregated residential patterns characteristic of middle- and high-income whites. Likewise, if racial discrimination and any other race-connected factors that affect housing choice were removed, segregation along economic lines could still persist.

Black disadvantages in educational attainment, in occupational achievement, and in income account for only a small amount of their observable segregation in urban space. The web of discrimination is a principal factor underlying racial segregation. The blacks have sharply limited options with respect to housing choices.

The conclusion to be drawn is significant: If a policy of socioeconomic mixing is to be pursued, the rationale must be something other than racial desegregation. Moreover, simultaneous efforts to reduce racial segregation and class stratification may in fact be counterproductive. Socioeconomic stratification warrants examination as a separate policy issue.

FINDING

> *While the low-income status of blacks is a factor in their segregation, race prejudice exerts a strong independent influence on the separation of the races.*

*   *   *

SOCIAL STRATIFICATION IN URBAN AREAS: THE BROAD PATTERN

The exact history of socioeconomic stratification in American cities remains uncertain. Research findings are incomplete. There are also discrepancies in discussions of present urban patterns. Hauser maintains that distance from the central city and socioeconomic status are directly related: The income level increases as one moves toward the urban fringe. Schnore's research basically supports that contention but points to the influence of factors such as city size, age, and regional location on the distribution of socioeconomic strata. However, suburban areas are not, and probably never were, uniformly of higher socioeconomic status than city districts. This is the thrust of the findings of Berger, of Dobriner, and of others who have studied working-class suburbs. These sources contend that suburban areas are more varied than is often acknowledged.

Nevertheless, most of the research done to date does support the view that socioeconomic stratification by residential location is widespread and persistent. Still in question are the exact patterns and tendencies of that stratification. One research finding, however, seems beyond dispute. Within metropolitan areas in every section of the country there are indeed significant socioeconomic differences between the populations of the central cities and those of the suburbs.

For urban Americans, a general rule may be stated as "The higher up the social ladder, the farther out you live." However, there are important variations. In many circumstances, the simple "distance from the urban center" description of differentiation hides a more complex reality. The search for an "evolutionary sequence" in the redistribution of social classes in American cities goes on, but the work of accurately describing the process, let alone comprehending the underlying forces at work, is still at an early stage. The effect of altering the process is uncertain. The criteria by which to evaluate and eventually choose among various alternatives are largely lacking.

Urban Americans have long been observed to "sift and sort" themselves in space in terms of three attributes: (1) social class (socioeconomic status), (2) color or ethnicity, and (3) type of family. Yet the nature and meaning of recent trends remain uncertain. Part of the difficulty is methodological. In the limited body of relevant research, there is (1) lack of consensus regarding the appropriate areal units, time intervals, and measures of "social class," (2) reliance on cross-sectional data for testing inherently longitudinal propositions, and (3) heavy dependence on case studies of individual urban areas, usually larger and older metropolitan complexes. There is further lack of consensus as to how measures of socioeconomic status are to be used and what may be inferred from them.

Three measures of socioeconomic status (or class) derive from census sources. These are (1) years of education, (2) occupation, and (3) income. All three measures are used for socioeconomic comparisons. However, there is limited agreement on the number of class strata that are meaningful. Neither is there widespread agreement on the values, beliefs, or behavior that are systematically to be associated with various strata. In the absence of an adequate description of the patterns and trends of social stratification, the development of reliable policy instruments for achieving socioeconomic residential mixing is problematic.

1722621

FINDING

> *In general, socioeconomic status rises with distance from the center of the metropolitan area. However, there are many contextual variations. The stratification process and the pattern that results are not yet well understood. Thus, the effect of efforts to alter the process is uncertain.*

*   *   *

IS SOCIOECONOMIC RESIDENTIAL MIXING DESIRABLE?

Here again social science by no means provides a conclusive answer. One viewpoint is that socioeconomic stratification is objectionable because it is "alien both to our traditions and to our concept of social progress." Stratification in low-income neighborhoods, according to this view, produces social and cultural isolation, which fosters and perpetuates defeatism. It is also argued, with more empirical support, that stratification affects the economic opportunities of inner-city residents because it makes their access to expanding industrial and commercial areas in the suburbs more costly. On the positive side, it is contended that class heterogeneity has (1) enriched the lives of the people; (2) promoted tolerance of social and cultural differences; (3) broadened the educational experience of children; and (4) encouraged exposure to alternative ways of life. Others have supported greater balance in the central city in the belief that an improved financial situation for the city would result. In other words, the problem as they see it is to attract the more affluent in order to improve the city's economic base. And still others see dispersal as "consistent with the stated goals of American society."

Not all observers are convinced that the ends sought can actually be accomplished through mixing. Some doubt that neighborhood heterogeneity does indeed produce tolerance and a more democratic order. Gans states, for example, that "A mixing of all age and class groups is likely to produce at best a polite but cool social climate, lacking the consensus and intensity of relations that are necessary for mutual enrichment." Others also question the assumption that geographical proximity enhances social interaction among disparate groups. Even when some socioeconomic balance is achieved, a highly interactive community need not result. Instead, small differences in population characteristics, such as occupation and education, may be given great emphasis, and association may be restricted to those who are "alike." Those who doubt the possibility or utility of balance do not oppose housing programs for the poor. However, they do raise the question as to whether housing and residential distribution is the most effective way to eliminate barriers to equal opportunity. They suggest it might be better to put the money into improvement of services for the underprivileged.

In sum, one can say with considerable certainty that if present trends continue unaltered, a pattern of socioeconomic stratification will persist. It is also certain that the arguments for and against socio-economic mixing are both diverse and lacking an adequate empirical base—but the question will increasingly arise: Should governments attempt to shape urban development, especially with reference to socioeconomic class phenomena?

FINDING

> *At present, the desirability of intervention to foster socioeconomic mixing in residential areas is uncertain. In question are not only the possible benefits but the untested assumptions concerning the amount and kind of present interaction across socioeconomic lines.*

*   *   *

IS SOCIOECONOMIC RESIDENTIAL MIXING FEASIBLE?

Assuming a policy of imposed socioeconomic residential mixing as desirable, is it feasible?

FINDING

> *There is no evidence from field studies that socioeconomic mixing is feasible. The trend in the movements of urban population is toward increasing separation of socioeconomic categories. The tendency is manifested among blacks as well as among whites.*

*   *   *

Taking note of the limits of present knowledge, a number of questions are posed. The intent is to sketch a framework for future investigation and research.

Housing Preferences　Our first set of questions has to do with the reasons people live where they do. In some respects the answer seems to be relatively clear. One barrier to economic heterogeneity in the suburbs, metropolitan or otherwise, is the cost of housing. Given restricted incomes, the lower class seeks housing it can afford. That housing is not likely to be found in middle-class neighborhoods whether they occur inside or outside central-city boundaries.

But why is low-cost housing excluded from those neighborhoods? Fears for safety and security and preference for certain life styles have, as noted above, led to restrictions on the construction of residences likely to serve lower-income persons. However, general concern for the maintenance of property and other values may be a more basic consideration.

Such considerations may account for the housing patterns of the poor, but how satisfactorily do they explain middle-income housing circumstances? Why do middle-class persons prefer suburban living? Because they cannot afford to live in the city? Because the city is for the very poor and the very rich? Or does the explanation lie in attitudes and beliefs? Glazer suggests that the desire to live among persons with similar interests, outlooks, and life styles leads middle-income people away from the lower class. Also, of course, lack of services and facilities may spur migration. Deterioration of school programs and city services may be both cause and effect of middle-class movements.

The housing preferences of all middle-class persons, of course, are not identical. There have always been some affluent families who have preferred central-city living. A recent Harris national survey found that a significant number of suburbanites would also prefer to live in small towns.

"Real Costs"　Another possibility may be that people tend to live where they do because, within the context of their life styles, the prices most important to them are lower, and therefore their "real income" is higher in the chosen locations. To illustrate, it may be that "real incomes" generally are lower at the urban fringe for those varieties of housing, transportation, and retailing valued by middle- and upper-income households. For them, the relative cost of living appears to be lower in the suburbs. Vacant land on prime sites is

available for new houses without incurring the cost of the purchase and demolition of an old building. Again, in theory, land prices are lower on the fringe by the amount of additional transportation cost incurred traveling to and from the center of town. However, speculation and other factors often distort land prices, and many people may no longer work in the center. Moreover, transportation costs to and from the center may be irrelevant for most people. Still, given that the well-to-do household will own one or two automobiles and will incur the fixed cost of that ownership for other reasons, and given the national propensity to subsidize the use of the automobile, the marginal transportation costs of automobile-owning households appear to favor the outermost parts of the central city and the suburbs even though the total cost is high. Large lots and automobiles are truly "complementary goods": A preference for space forces dependence on the automobile and a preference for the automobile forces a spreading out.

Conversely, is the central city, and the inner city in particular, the cheapest place, at least in out-of-pocket costs, for lower-income people to live? Nowhere else is the supply of old (cheap) housing as large, especially rental housing. Public transportation services are offered to more places and with less delay than in any other part of the urban area. Under existing conditions real-cost transportation savings accrue to the users of public transportation because of residential clustering. Moreover, the larger the number of low-income households that are massed in the market area of a retail business district, the more likely it is that there will be cheap restaurants, "dime" stores, laundromats, barber colleges, and other such facilities. Given the relative immobility of the poor, only spatial massing may provide one of these facilities nearby and another similar shop not too much farther away for some semblance of competition in retailing, even when the prices are relatively high compared with those in large outlets in the suburbs.

If these differential advantages do in fact exist, what are the implications for policy? Must they be accepted as given? Or, if not, what are the considerations and costs involved in their modification?

Public Sector Costs   What role does the distribution of public sector costs play in reinforcing existing patterns of residential choice? Ideally, government provides an array of services and pays for these services by taxation, user charges, or borrowing. On the one hand, government provides for planned transfer payments; on the other, it seeks to prevent unplanned transfers resulting in inequitable sharing of the costs of public services. Accordingly, taxes and services bear close inspection to be sure that they are not giving out antisocial signals, that is to say, encouraging unplanned transfers.

When asked to give their reasons for moving out of the central city, more than 60 percent of the people said they believed they could get more housing space for the money. A substantial number mentioned the crowded conditions in the city. Only 3 percent mentioned taxes as a reason. Actually, people seem to be willing to pay more to live in suburban areas. They prefer the space and find suburbia a better place to raise children. By and large, they do not seem to have precise knowledge of the services they receive for their tax dollar. Precise comparisons of tax levels and the quality of services received appear to be infrequent. It must be noted that suburban residence is not limited to the middle- and the upper-middle classes. For example, many blue-collar workers now are suburban residents. Indeed, the people at the top of each income or educational stratum tend to move and consistently these moves are toward the suburbs.

Of course, some middle- and upper-income people may be induced to select suburban residential sites because the tax-price of providing public services is lower in the area. Given existing commitments to render income-redistributive services, then residential site selection designed to minimize one's contribution to these transfer payments becomes a simple zero-sum game—if I win, you lose. In relation to the central-city tax base, however, industry and commerce, which account for up to 70 percent of revenues, are much more significant. Many, perhaps most, inner-city areas are not yielding revenues comparable with the costs they generate. And in blighted areas in seven cities studied, costs exceeded revenues in ratios ranging from 2.2 to 1.0 to as high as 9.1 to 1.0. In another study, the National Association of Home Builders found that city slums were generating 45 percent of the costs but only 6 percent of the revenues.

Finally, it is important to note that the density of urban settlements appears to be declining in all parts of the country. In making a residential choice, individuals may seek to strike a balance between money costs and benefits and real costs and benefits. The choice is mediated by many factors—not simply by money costs. As in other areas of modern society, the sum of individual satisfaction needs to be assessed in light of the social costs of the individual choices. In this regard, attitude studies designed to evaluate the complete range of human needs and priorities would be helpful.

One approach to the allocation of these additional costs may be to shift the burden of major public functions to a higher level of government. Indeed, this process seems to be under way. In the short run, however, movement of industry, commerce, and middle- and upper-income families to the suburbs tends to impoverish the central cities by undermining their fiscal capacity. In the longer run, the effect seems likely to be a shifting of the financial responsibility for the support and development of low-income families from local to state and federal levels. In short, it may be the most politically expedient way to transfer the financing of health, education, and welfare from the less appropriate property tax to the more appropriate income tax.

Correcting the price incidence of services could also be achieved in part by special measures such as impact grants to suburban communities as an incentive to accept larger numbers of minority or lower-income families. Alternatively, costly public services such as education or welfare could be more fully financed by states or the federal government according to formulae that would take into account both the total population of a community and the burdens placed upon it by its income distribution, its property-base mix, and the numbers of children to be educated.

Changes in the tax structure of local jurisdictions provide, in theory at least, an alternative approach to changing the calculus of costs and benefits.

Most local units of government in metropolitan areas rely primarily on the property tax. The burden of residential property taxes has been extensively studied. In brief, such taxes fall heavily on housing consumers. Further, these taxes may fall proportionately more heavily on renters (as increased rents) than on home owners who may be able to take offsetting income tax deductions.

Some communities offering high levels of service may have such a favorable property-tax base (e.g., high valuation of commercial, industrial, or residential property) that they can maintain relatively low tax rates. And where tax disparities exist between local communities, the ones with low taxes sometimes succeed in attracting even more economic activity, thereby reinforcing their favorable situation.

Income taxes are not typically used by local governments, although there is a trend toward their use, especially by cities. Income taxes, by whatever jurisdiction levied, have an impact on housing. They favor owners of housing; conversely, they discriminate against renters. Because of the depreciation formulae permitted, income-tax provisions also favor the owners of rental property. Gains in property transactions can be taxed at capital-gains rates; losses can be fully deductible. In his report to the Douglass Commission, Slitor outlined various proposals for tax reform, while still respecting the overall value of the income tax. A major consideration for local communities is the extent to which the income tax can be used to supplement the property tax.

Subsidies It is important to try to eliminate unplanned transfer payments from the relative price structure so that the advantage of behavior that has acted to pull the income classes apart—movement to the suburbs—is eliminated. Only then is it prudent to attempt to introduce a set of subsidies designed to bring them back together. Neutralizing subsidies are uncertain in effect and expensive. To illustrate, we are now beginning a billion-dollar-a-year federal mass-transit grant program to offset the effects of years of automobile subsidization. Offsetting subsidies exhaust the scarce supply of tax money. Even if transfer payments are arranged properly, however, there may still be real-cost differences left that would tend to favor clustering by socioeconomic class, especially by income.

In sum, to achieve the highest social welfare, it may be in order to weigh the lower private costs of residential stratification against the social benefits of residential mixing. Offering money rewards for a social benefit is what we are doing in effect when we restrict federal grants for urban infrastructure, as in the New Town legislation, to only those communities that make provision for housing a *pro rata* share of low-income households. Of course, more fundamental action than any now being considered may be required if we seek to alter the price and preference structure that presently governs residential choice.

FINDING

> *A more adequate knowledge base is needed in order to determine the feasibility of socioeconomic residential mixing. More information is needed about why people live where they do and, specifically, about (1) housing preferences and attitudes; (2) "real costs" for different socioeconomic groups; (3) public sector costs and benefits, both perceived and actual; (4) alternative approaches to correcting public sector costs and changing individual "real costs"; and (5) the "human costs" of socioeconomic stratification.*

Employment Opportunity Costs   An unplanned transfer payment of
a different kind may result from the dispersion of employment opportunities. A great deal of evidence has been accumulated on the shift
in the distribution of employment within metropolitan areas. In every
area studied, almost all recent employment growth has taken place in
the suburban ring and not in the central city. Close analysis shows a
serious imbalance resulting from this shift.

As many types of jobs move into the periphery, the central cities are becoming
more and more specialized in functions which require chiefly professional, technical and clerical workers—a skilled and literate labor force. But the skilled and
literate groups are precisely those segments of the population which are increasingly choosing to live outside the urban center. The slum dwellers, on the other
hand, are poorly suited to fill the city's office and service jobs; the jobs for which
they are suited—the less skilled occupations involved in many types of manufac-
turing, wholesaling, and household service operations—are moving farther and
farther away from them.[8]

The importance of one's housing as the locational base from which
one has access to employment and other services is stressed by various
reports. As the Kaiser Committee put it:

The location of one's place of residence determines the accessibility and quality
of many everyday advantages taken for granted by the mainstream of American
society. Among these commonplace advantages are public educational facilities
for a family's children, adequate police and fire protection, and a decent sur-
rounding environment. In any case, a family should have a choice of living as
close as economically possible to the breadwinner's place of employment.[9]

Segregated residential patterns impair the effective operation of
the labor markets. In one major metropolitan area, for example,
studies have shown that in every major occupation, the farther one
moves from the concentrated minority population, the smaller the
percentage of minority workers in each occupation.

Transportation is an integral feature of the spatial structure of a
community, providing both services within the community and links
to more distant points. Transportation facilities do not offer equal
services to advantaged and disadvantaged persons. In particular, com-
muter systems that satisfactorily bring workers into the metropolitan
center are not geared to take low-income workers to jobs in the suburbs with equal effectiveness. This discrepancy is largely due to the
lack of congruence of the spatial spread of places of employment in
the suburban area and the existing public transportation systems. In
any event, additional costs in time, or money, must be borne by

central-city residents. Residential dispersal might facilitate increased access to employment opportunities, but the advantage would be mainly limited to those who could drive to work. In the suburbs, workers rarely live within walking distance of jobs, and low density makes for poor lateral public transport. For those with the least skills, either continued clustering of jobs and residences for channeled movement or new forms of subsidized transport will be needed.

FINDING

> *Stratification by socioeconomic characteristics, as with segregation by race, tends to raise the employment opportunity costs of workers least able to bear costs. Such costs are being lowered, however, by the suburbanization of blue-collar workers.*

*   *   *

Governmental Fragmentation Autonomous local government units within a metropolitan area often appear to comport themselves like business firms; that is, their officials weigh public actions on behalf of their communities so as to create the most favorable balance between returns from revenue and expenditures for services. They tend to equate fiscal protectionism with responsible leadership. Fiscal considerations lie behind policies purporting to preserve the character of the community and to order its physical arrangement but that subtly fuse into less openly stated policies designed to keep out low-income or minority families.

There is a need to understand where support for or resistance to residential dispersal and integration is most likely to be generated—whether from elected governmental officials, governmental staff members, nongovernmental organizations, or selected individual citizens. For example, it may be important to examine thoroughly the role of the realtor in reflecting and shaping community opinion. A study of Kalamazoo (although not a suburban city) showed that realtors were able to exercise a degree of influence beyond their presumed strength in defeating a proposal to create a city housing commission. What other key groups are in a position to "make or break" programs that would increase housing options?

Local autonomy, some analysts suggest, may help to ensure a range of choice for metropolitan residents who can choose the particular level and character of services they want and can afford. However, the literature is not at all clear on when quantity and quality differentials in local public services, characteristic of local political fragmentation, are in the social interest and when they are not, that is, when uniform standards are "better."

If local political fragmentation has a cost that we wish to minimize, a base for a new brand of leadership will be needed in most metropolitan areas. Councils of government, having spread rapidly during recent years, characteristically lack political muscle and may, in fact, be better designed to block rather than to give informed leadership in steps toward effective metropolitan government. The federal and state governments may initiate programs and provide financial support, but the allocation of housing responsibilities within a given metropolitan area must be undertaken at the local, albeit metropolitan, level.

FINDING

> *Local government autonomy in metropolitan areas results in an uneven distribution of public sector costs; some government units are forced to assume the costs of decisions and policies adopted by other units.*

5

Urban Development: Research, Evaluation, and Experimentation

Urban populations, viewed locality by locality, tend to be economically stratified. At the same time, metropolitan areas, seen as a whole, exhibit considerable heterogeneity. While there appears to be a tendency for economic status to rise with distance from the heart of the central city, metropolitan areas exhibit considerable diversity of pattern. Moreover, many urban localities manifest segregated patterns of living, yet the distribution of minority populations tends to follow, in a more confined area, the pattern of economic stratification characteristic of the white population. Existing knowledge in which one can have a high degree of confidence is insufficient with respect to the dynamics of urban development and stratification. We do not know with enough exactitude

- The historical patterns of development and stratification that have characterized urban areas;
- The factors and forces that underlie and shape urban development;
- The effectiveness of the institutions that influence the pattern of urban development;
- The institutions that comprise a "web of discrimination," reinforcing patterns of segregation;
- The social–psychological and other factors that affect residential choice;
- The measurable effects of continued stratification, on the one hand, or of a change to residential mixing, on the other; and

• Finally, in the absence of experimentation on a substantial scale, we do not have the knowledge needed to make informed choices among alternative patterns of development.

Decisions must inevitably be made even in the face of uncertainty and imperfect knowledge. We do not suggest that they wait. In our judgment, however, the creation of a comprehensive and systematic knowledge base for community development and housing programs is a critical and urgent need. Without attempting to delineate all the parameters of such a comprehensive effort, we can identify certain priority requirements. These research, evaluation, and experimental priority elements are briefly described below.

Urban Development Patterns   A better historical understanding of the main trends of urban development through 1970 is essential. In particular, a better appreciation of the possible diversity of the patterns of stratification—their heterogeneity and homogeneity—is needed.

• Longitudinally oriented studies of the main trends in urban development should be undertaken. The time periods studied must be much longer than those to which social scientists have ordinarily directed their attention. Too often generalizations have been made about "trends" of urban development from segments of upswings or downswings. These studies should be facilitated by regional data analysis and processing centers designed, on the one hand, to contribute to the increase of the productivity of the independent research workers and, on the other hand, to be responsive to the inquiries of policy makers.
• Federal research funds should be available to encourage research that
      Has a metropolitan-wide context—including central city, suburbs, rural–urban fringe and rural territory;
      Includes simultaneous observations of both racial and class characteristics;
      Throws light on hitherto unexplored characteristics of annexed areas and suburbs; and
      Utilizes the new 1970 data in replication of selected prior research of significance.
• Most importantly, support should be provided for research that seeks to provide an understanding of the diversity of the patterns of distribution of various socioeconomic strata within metropolitan areas.

Forces Underlying Metropolitan Development   A considerable body of research has been concerned with the factors that relate to why one urban area or region develops rather than another. In contrast, the research devoted to understanding the "forces" that shape the pattern of development within metropolitan areas is negligible. A number of urban simulation models designed to throw light on some of the major policy choices are being designed and tested. While potentially valuable, they are likely to raise more questions than they answer. In addition a firmly grounded conceptual and empirical base is needed to provide verifiable propositions and the data with which to do so.

• One major requirement is to obtain a more complete and explicit understanding of the internal metropolitan price structure, which provides the context for an array of private and public decisions.

What, for example, are the cost-of-living differentials for low-income as compared with high-income families in the central city and in the suburbs? What part of the variation is a "real cost" in transportation (access) or living amenities? What part is a private advantage won by flight?

How does implicit social pricing as reflected in such services as education and welfare and in such revenue measures as local property and income taxes influence residential choice and the policy of local public bodies?

What are the cost–benefit tradeoffs of employment opportunity, transportation, and residential location for various economic strata?

What are the second-order effects of changes in manufacturing-service ratios and changes in their spatial distribution within the metropolitan area?

And finally, are urban characteristics such as size and physical density simply descriptive or are they surrogates for important factors such as crowding?

Strategic Nodes in the Web of Discrimination   Stable interracial living requires behavioral change in many of the institutions concerned with the housing market, which now act in a discriminatory fashion. Research on how these various elements perform their services has been limited. Analysis done with an eye to identifying the points at which intervention may be most effective is needed.

The planning, actual production, and subsequent sale and resale or rental of housing are a complex set of subprocesses with innumerable constraints, regulations, and negotiations among various parties at sequential points. Given this complexity and the number of points at which behind-the-scenes negotiations and decisions may occur, it is difficult to pinpoint discrimination as such so that steps can be taken to eliminate it. Incentives need to be designed that make selling to minorities attractive to brokers and sellers.

Discrimination is most visible at the actual point of sale or rental of housing. A real estate broker or a management agent may become a crucial gatekeeper at that point, and it is the point at which fair-housing laws seek to eliminate discrimination. But for all its importance, it is merely the most visible step in a much larger institutional structure.

Available research literature does not show clearly the points at which discrimination can be most effectively attacked and suburban communities encouraged or forced to admit minority households. There are no simple strategies. Approaches are needed that go well beyond antidiscrimination. The web of discrimination is so complex that a multifaceted effort—using fiscal, legal, and political means—must be made.

Studies are needed to isolate the interrelated urban subsystems that regulate land development and utilization and demonstrate how the subsystems work. These studies would incorporate an examination of the performance of

Brokers
Real estate boards
Appraisers
Developers—small and large
Mortgage lenders
Local government
    Zoning
    Subdivision controls
    Land-use planning

Finally, evaluation of the positive and negative consequences with respect to social mixing of various federal programs is needed. These include

Rental subsidies
Owner subsidies
Urban renewal
Comprehensive planning
Model cities
FHA mortgage guarantees

Social–Psychological Factors in Housing   Race is just one of many factors involved in residential choice, and it is often not a critical one for either whites or blacks. Many other factors are taken into account in housing selection. Some of these are location convenient to work, appropriate-sized dwelling unit, special features such as style, and financial advantages. While some of the factors in residential choice are known in a general way, present knowledge does not provide a reliable basis for policies and programs. The social psychology of housing choice deserves increased research attention. Studies are needed that examine common assumptions with respect to

- Harmful effects of residential stratification;
- Measurable effects of social mixing; and
- Consequences of improvements in the quality of housing.

Beyond these specific suggestions, the most important need is for broad behavioral and motivational research on the people themselves. What are the behavioral and attitudinal causes of pressing urban problems? What do different groups really want? How can the clarification of their objectives be facilitated? In this connection there is need for preparation of a manual for "Effective Community Action" in housing.

Review of the Literature   In the present study, the "state of the knowledge" literature review by established scholars has proved to be very valuable. A similar approach to other areas could prove useful to HUD. A review of the literature is suggested with respect to

- Housing choices of nonblack groups of Americans of Mexican, Puerto Rican, Cuban, and Indian origin;
- Implication of socioeconomic class differences for American democratic society; and
- Implications for U.S. housing policy of the emerging emphasis on "alternative life styles."

Alternative Methods of Achieving Equal Opportunity   Residential mixing is only one approach to the attainment of equal opportunity. Other approaches, such as substantial improvement in the services provided to central-city residents, need to be examined on a comparative cost–benefit basis. If several approaches prove feasible, priorities need to be determined.

Experimentation—"New Living Arrangements" Innovative development of new communities with unconventional residency patterns could have the effect of changing tasks and demand patterns. A new community is an indivisible entity and presents problems similar to those treated in the theoretical considerations of the private sector versus the public sector. Classical economics was concerned with the goods that could be produced in small outputs at reasonable costs— the factors of production were divisible and the outputs highly divisible. For example, in the production of consumer goods, it became possible to satisfy minority tastes at reasonable cost. There are cases, however, such as the choice of transportation, which cannot be so accommodated. If 80 percent of the people have become adjusted to traveling by auto, there is in most cases no reasonable economic way to produce public transportation for the other 20 percent because of the indivisibility of the heavy fixed investment.

Similarly, the development of new communities that feature built-in opportunities for social mixing—racial and economic—can be viewed as an indivisible good. Individual choice is limited unless such new communities exist. To bring them into being, it may be necessary for the government to adopt an experimental approach and, in effect, to take the lead in joint ventures with the private sector. Experimentation of this nature may lead to changes in demand patterns, but, more importantly, it may lead to the identification of significant unsatisfied demand that already regards heterogeneity as desirable. HUD now has an active New Towns program. However, a wide range of experimentation with adequate provision for systematic evaluation deserves to be considered.

Scale is a critical variable in the elaboration of any policy of social mixing. The implications may be very different at the family, neighborhood, and community scales. Therefore, experimentation is needed at several levels—the physical building, the block, the neighborhood, the school district, the high school district, and the full-scale new community. In the latter case, experiments with several main types are desirable. One is the metropolitan industrial satellite that is designed to be a net importer of labor and a net exporter of goods and services. The second is the relatively remote and self-contained suburb that in fact remains a net exporter of labor, professional or otherwise. A third might be a large central-city development that encompasses working and recreation, as well as residential, areas.

With respect to economic mixing, these experiments, in addition to clarifying questions of the feasibility of mixing on different scales, could help to answer questions such as

What can be done to shift taste patterns and thereby change effective demand in a socially beneficial direction?

How many levels up the housing and residence scale is it feasible to move lower-income familities?

Is it most effective to subsidize those with low income into a high-rent district or to subsidize the up-grading of the social capital (infrastructure) and public services so necessary to induce those with higher incomes to relocate (or stay) in the older (poorer) sections of the metropolitan area?

In sum, we conclude that experimental developments in different locations and on different scales are needed to test potential demand patterns and to assist in providing the necessary knowledge base for national community development and housing policies. Experiments should be carefully designed to test a specific range of issues. Then, provision must be made for independent evaluation of the outcomes.

FINDING

> *Experiments in socioeconomic mixing at a number of different scales could help to provide a better basis for policy formulation. The same procedure would be valuable with respect to racial mixing.*

References

1. John H. Denton, *Report of Consultant* (San Francisco: National Committee Against Discrimination in Housing, 1970, Appendix J of Summary Report by NCDH).
2. Eleanor Leacock *et al.*, *Toward Integration in Suburban Housing: The Bridgeview Study* (Washington, D.C.: B'nai B'rith, 1965), p. 32.
3. John H. Denton, *Report of Consultant* (San Francisco: National Committee Against Discrimination in Housing, 1970, Appendix J of Summary Report by NCDH).
4. Davis McEntire, *Residence and Race* (Berkeley and Los Angeles: University of California Press, 1960), pp. 218–219.
5. John H. Denton, *Report of Consultant* (San Francisco: National Committee Against Discrimination in Housing, 1970, Appendix J of Summary Report by NCDH), p. 32.
6. Philip P. Green, Jr., "Land Subdivision," in William I. Goodman and Eric C. Freund (eds.), *Principles and Practice of Urban Planning* (Chicago: International City Managers Association, 1968), p. 449.
7. Karl E. and Alma F. Taeuber, *Negroes in Cities* (Chicago: Aldine Press, 1965) pp. 94–95.
8. Benjamin Chinitz (ed.), *City and Suburbs: The Economics of Metropolitan Growth* (Englewood Cliffs, New Jersey: Prentice Hall, 1964), pp. 28–29.
9. The President's Committee on Urban Housing [the Kaiser Committee], *A Decent Home* (Washington, D.C.: Government Printing Office, 1968), p. 13.

RECOMMENDATIONS OF THE ADVISORY COMMITTEE

Part II of the report, *Freedom of Choice in Housing: Opportunities and Constraints*, contains the policy and research recommendations of the Advisory Committee to the Department of Housing and Urban Development. Each of the twelve recommendations is preceded by a summary statement intended to provide an explanatory context.

Recommendations of the Advisory Committee to the Department of Housing and Urban Development

The objectives of HUD social policy as stated by HUD officials are three:

- To increase the options of minorities;
- To alter attitudes in directions favorable to desegregation; and
- To improve the quality of the environment of low- and moderate-income groups.

HUD is also concerned with meeting a number of housing production objectives. The combined social and production objectives have led in practice to the concept of "social mixing" in both the suburbs and central cities.

Social mixing does not refer to recreation or leisure-time interaction, but rather to social diversity in residential areas. "Mixing" may mean either racially mixed neighborhoods and communities or economically mixed communities, or a combination of both. However, the problems that arise and the institutions that must be mobilized to achieve one or another of these outcomes may be very different.

- Interracial neighborhood and housing units are feasible. Evidence to support this proposition is both varied and conclusive.
- Knowledge of the feasibility of mixing of people of different economic levels in the same relatively small residential areas or housing units is both inadequate and inconclusive. However, we know of

at least one promising experiment that combines economic and racial mixing.

- In the 1960's, the income gap between white and black American families narrowed markedly.
- Racially mixed neighborhoods, including those into which both whites and blacks are currently moving, are numerous and widespread in the United States.
- At the same time, available evidence suggests that, since 1940, the nation's housing has become more, not less, segregated by race.

RECOMMENDATION 1

> *Initially, in light of the conclusive evidence on its feasibility, the primary emphasis of a policy of social diversity in housing should be on opening options for racial mixing of those with corresponding economic capabilities. At the same time, we recognize the importance of the issue of economic mixing and urge support for high-priority experimental and research programs to create an adequate knowledge base for policies in that area.*

*   *   *

The *scale* and *pattern* on which the mixing of residences of persons of different income levels and of different racial or ethnic identities is attempted are important and insufficiently understood variables. These variables affect both the initial feasibility of alternative sites and the probable stability of the social mix once attained.

The reason for a policy of residential mixing is also a factor. On the one hand, in racial mixing the primary objective may be to increase options and to reduce prejudice. On the other hand, the objective of economic mixing may be primarily to distribute the large concentration of low-income families more widely throughout the metropolitan area in order to facilitate access to employment opportunities and improve the quality of their environment. Inferences with respect to social mixing may be quite different for random next-door relations in neighborhoods than with respect to aggregations of housing predominantly occupied by one race in the high school district, the suburb, or the "new town."

RECOMMENDATION 2

> *Carefully planned experiments on a number of different scales and patterns from the neighborhood to the new town should*

be undertaken to determine the conditions under which residential mixing of families or individuals of different racial and economic categories may be most feasible.

*   *   *

Multiple factors determine the extent and stability of interracial residential areas. These include

- Levels of tolerance and prejudice;
- Relative demand for housing among the white majority and the minorities;
- Supply of housing, both the actual physical supply and the "effective" supply taking into account an array of institutional barriers to equal access; and
- Local, state, and federal government policies and programs that may impede or facilitate the creation of an adequate supply of housing and equal access to it.

RECOMMENDATION 3

Barriers to stable interracial neighborhoods and housing are numerous and pervasive. No single factor approach will result in substantial improvement. It is essential that HUD pursue a multiple strategy that takes account of the interplay of all the factors in the market as they are modified by prejudice. Undergirding the strategy must be enforcement of the law to a single standard—the attainment of one open housing market, not two (or more) segregated markets.

*   *   *

The extent of willingness among whites and among blacks to accept residential racial mixing appears to be widely misperceived.

- Racial intolerance among Americans is steadily decreasing in the area of housing, as well as in many others.
- The percentage of white respondents who report they would not mind having black neighbors more than doubled from 1942 to 1968 (35 to 76 percent).
- When presented with a meaningful choice between an all-black neighborhood and a mixed neighborhood, blacks overwhelmingly favor the latter.

RECOMMENDATION 4

*To provide a better basis for policy formulation and imple-
mentation, the federal government should support survey research on attitudes toward racial and economic residential
diversity on a regular and comparable basis.*

*   *   *

More tolerant or accepting white attitudes have not been reflected in
behavioral change in the housing area to as great an extent as in other
areas of race relations. Four factors help to explain the difference:

• The fact that prejudice among whites need not be strong enough
to generate active resistance to racial mixing in order to produce a
segregated outcome over time;
• The perceived "closeness" of racial mixing in housing as compared with areas like employment;
• The relatively limited optimal contact between members of the
majority and minorities in the housing area; and
• The relative dearth of effective neighborhood organizations
sanctioning interracial living.

RECOMMENDATION 5

*In order to achieve stable racial mixing in neighborhoods and
housing units, policy must not only aim at overcoming initial
resistance but at reducing the role of discrimination to a point
that will permit retention and replacement of both majority
and minority residents. To the maximum degree feasible, specific actions to permit residential racial mixing should be ac-
companied by the creation of local groups to improve com-
munication and sanction desegregation.*

*   *   *

Behavior change in intergroup relations typically precedes rather than
follows attitude change. This proposition is significant for public policy at all levels.

• Success in interracial contact depends on specific conditions.
Prejudice is lessened when two groups

Possess equal status;

Seek common goals;
Are interdependent;
Interact with the positive support of authority, law, or custom.

• An effective way to alter opposition, white and minority, to interracial housing is to have both groups live successfully in such housing.

RECOMMENDATION 6

> *Policies designed to achieve racially mixed neighborhoods and housing should aim at providing the physical and social environment for constructive contact conditions for all groups.*

*   *   *

The stability and, in the longer run, the existence of racially mixed neighborhoods depend on the relationship between racial proportions among existing residents and entrants.

• Stability in racially mixed neighborhoods can be achieved at many different ratios of white to nonwhite occupancy.
• If stability is to be maintained, white home seekers must not avoid housing that represents good value for the money just because of nonwhite entry.
• Minority demand must not be so strong and focused as to absorb all or nearly all the housing that becomes available in a particular area.
• In many areas a factor of group dominance must be taken into account.
• The microlevel policies of those who manage or sell housing can greatly influence racial proportions in different neighborhoods.

RECOMMENDATION 7

> *While opposing the use of rigid quotas, managements should be encouraged to adopt flexible intervention policies to foster stable interracial neighborhoods.*

*   *   *

An adequate supply of good-quality housing that is also a good value for the money is important in achieving and maintaining interracial neighborhoods.

- Both persons who prefer integration and those who prefer segregation tend to place physical considerations and convenience ahead of racial preferences.
- Racial mixing is feasible at all price levels, but stable and substantial mixing is most possible in the middle price range.
- Residential location in relation to employment is an important factor in housing choice.

RECOMMENDATION 8

> *Federal policy should continue to emphasize the expansion of the supply of good-quality housing for all economic groups conveniently located in relation to where job opportunities exist or can be created, whether in the suburbs or the central city.*

*   *   *

The "effective" supply of good-quality housing is reduced by a web of institutional discrimination. Private "gatekeepers" making up this web may include housing owners or managers, real estate brokers, real estate board developers, appraisers, and lending institutions.

RECOMMENDATION 9

> *Comprehensive government action is required to strengthen the processes and facilities necessary to achieve a single open market in housing and to ensure "fair shopping" conditions. Action required includes*
>
> - *Positive assistance for minority home seekers;*
> - *Positive incentives for housing middlemen to operate in a manner that encourages stable racial mixing; and*
> - *Measures to ensure equal access to real estate board listings throughout the metropolitan area. This may involve the creation of new marketing institutions.*

*   *   *

Rental housing, because of its wide accessibility, is a crucial area for the development of interracial housing.

- Rental housing, no matter how desirable and advantageous home ownership may be, remains the immediate prospect for most minority families.

• A considerable volume of good-quality rental housing convenient to new employment opportunities has been built in the last decade.

• Managers of rental property are more open to pressure and persuasion than are a multitude of individual home owners, and, once racial mixing is accepted, they can do much to ensure its stability.

RECOMMENDATION 10

> *Priority should be given to (1) an effort to open up suitable rental housing properties so situated as to elicit continuing demand from both whites and minorities; (2) programs to induce managements of rental properties to pursue an open housing policy and to inform them of practical means of carrying out such a policy.*

*   *   *

Discrimination in the sale of housing is evident in concern about property values and in the behavior of owners, brokers, and some developers.

• The weight of evidence is that, in comparison with similar all-white neighborhoods, property values in areas entered by nonwhites do not generally fall.

• Real estate brokers, despite fair-housing laws and policies, continue to screen home seekers on the basis of race.

• Policies of large firms of home builders toward racial mixing have become more affirmative. Changes in the policies of large developers can be very significant.

• However, progress in other sectors of the market is also essential to open up opportunities for minority families along the chain of moves resulting from the occupancy of new housing.

RECOMMENDATION 11

> *The programs of large developers who adopt positive management practices in support of an open housing policy are important, in terms of both scale and precedent, and should be facilitated.*

*   *   *

Local governments have commonly used a number of their delegated powers over land use and construction to resist initiatives that they view as leading to residential mixing, whether racial or economic. These powers include

- Zoning in which social influences more than economic considerations motivate public decision-makers;
- Subdivision regulation that controls the process by which land is converted to building sites; and
- Land-use plans that have tended to focus on "physical development" and have rarely sought to deal directly with housing requirements.

RECOMMENDATION 12

Major responsibility and authority for an adequate and equitably distributed supply of housing should be lodged at the metropolitan or state level. All federal programs should be administered to strengthen and encourage metropolitan and state leadership in carrying out this responsibility.